T0273064

DAY UNTO DAY

ALSO BY MARTHA COLLINS

POETRY

White Papers
Blue Front
Some Things Words Can Do
A History of Small Life on a Windy Planet
The Arrangement of Space
The Catastrophe of Rainbows

POETRY CHAPBOOKS

Sheer

Gone So Far

TRANSLATIONS

Black Stars: Poems by Ngo Tu Lap
(co-translated with the author)
Green Rice: Poems by Lam Thi My Da
(co-translated with Thuy Dinh)
The Women Carry River Water: Poems by Nguyen Quang Thieu
(co-translated with the author)

EDITED BOOK

Critical Essays on Louise Bogan

DAY UNTO DAY

Poems

MARTHA COLLINS

MILKWEED EDITIONS

Published 2014 by Milkweed Editions
Printed in Canada
Cover design by Gretchen Achilles/Wavetrap Design
Cover art by Jane Fulton Alt
Author photo by Doug Macomber
17   18   19   20   5   4   3   2
First Edition

Milkweed Editions, an independent nonprofit publisher, gratefully acknowledges
sustaining support from the Bush Foundation; the Patrick and Aimee Butler Foundation;
the Driscoll Foundation; the Jerome Foundation; the Lindquist & Vennum Foundation;
the McKnight Foundation; the National Endowment for the Arts; the Target Foundation;
and other generous contributions from foundations, corporations, and individuals. Also,
this activity is made possible by the voters of Minnesota through a Minnesota State Arts
Board Operating Support grant, thanks to a legislative appropriation from the arts and
cultural heritage fund, and a grant from the Wells Fargo Foundation Minnesota. For a
full listing of Milkweed Editions supporters, please visit milkweed.org.

Library of Congress Cataloging-in-Publication Data

Collins, Martha, 1940-
[Poems. Selections]
Day unto day : poems / Martha Collins. — First Edition.
    pages cm
ISBN 978-1-57131-452-9 (paperback : alk. paper) — ISBN 978-1-57131-848-0
(ebook)
I. Title.
PS3553.O4752A6 2014
811'.54--dc23

                    2013045896

Milkweed Editions is committed to ecological stewardship. We strive to align our book
production practices with this principle, and to reduce the impact of our operations in
the environment. We are a member of the Green Press Initiative, a nonprofit coalition
of publishers, manufacturers, and authors working to protect the world's endangered
forests and conserve natural resources. *Day Unto Day* was printed on acid-free 100%
postconsumer-waste paper by Friesens Corporation.

for Ted

CONTENTS

Day unto day uttereth speech,
and night unto night sheweth knowledge.

—*Psalm 19:2*

To live's a Gift, to dye's a Debt that we
Each of us owe unto Mortality.

—PHILIP PAIN, *Daily Meditations* (1668)

OVER TIME

OVER TIME

October 2004

1

Not much. Less. Slip
of a finger, diminished
interval, maybe third

of three or two.

Water mirrors house with high
green door opening out (no

steps) into pure air.

2

Air pockets three
hawks. Cat got
the bird got the cat.

Overflown. A habit
of flight. Worn cloud
on the edge of edge.

Wisps. Little tongues.

3

Tongues at work. *Talk Today*

She could did for an hour or more.

My first her, who gave me words.

Then at the end, before, merely Oh!

A moment of . . . of more, perhaps.

Oh sweet and blessèd could be.

Oh my soul

4

Soul slept, called in sick.

Late sun clouds
the lake with clouds.

Katydid down
to *–did –did*.

Nothing to be done.

Little sun, quarter moon.

5

Moon covered, un-
covered, covered again, cold.

Cold and hot, very and both.

Disturbed the Sea of Tranquility.

Distributed by the Moon Shop.

Distributed self in pieces.

Oh my broken.

6

Broken down, or out, as in
war, or into, soon: my own him.

How much we carry around
under our skins, many
we were, girls and boys

Now now

And then then.

7

Then gone and then to come:
all the time, except the split
second, except—

All the time in the world.

And out of this world?

Oh little heart on my wrist,
where are we going?

8

Going home: packed her bags
to go back ninety years

burning skirt broken fork
slow train the old house

current counter under cross

The one who gave me time

is out of time.

9

Time to shut the rattling
windows slamming doors

And if at first you don't and if
you try again and don't you
slip a little slide

Rope burns hands over
the book the pages over

10

Over time she—
Overtime. Timer
she was Click I mean

I. Would work the week
long song bird in the—

Burning bush ahead, red
sumac jeweled by sun.

11

Sun, here come the clouds
again. Between us. You

could care: you'll swallow
us up on your way out.

You're almost halfway
there, and here

am I, way past half.

12

Half-life, half-light, half-
moon, half-mast: low

flag, and every evening down.

Discovered a world of green
in him, on the shore
of newfound skin

His different hand

13

Hand over hand
over: change
for an empty

Enter the bare page

Oh keep him safe
in his thin shift
on his metal bed

14

Bed for one, my very
one, own, oh let

him let him

Someone's deep inside
him now, something

inside him's taken is
it is he let him breathe

15

Breathe light hold
in the light: him at bandaged
rest, her last year in her

last bed: the apple pink
just under the skin: I

am floating again a little less
less the chord resolving.

16

Resolved, that leaves should turn

and turn: color to motion to rest.

Flutter of yellow, flash of red, bronze-

leafed trunk fallen across the path.

Ducks twitch white tails over the water,

geese stretch necks . . . All fall down.

All rise. All different.

17

Different from us. Dry,
quiet. Still. Still

Freeman   Sarah   Rebekah   John

locust   maple   hornbeam   oak

Timothy. Bent grass under
our feet, over their bones.

Katheryn. Out of. Under and over.

18

Over my— my tiny
planet, growing colder, little

train that could but where's
the track?   On, *off*

again, over my, un-
done, nerve

flinched at No. But maybe If—

19

If. Only. Then
again. But out

of time just now as
the lace of yellow locust

leaves molecules
particles waves catches

its breath begins to hum.

20

Hum of words
under words: brief
for breath, him

for hum, him still
in his bed for one—

And clouds so thick and fast
the whole sky's turning.

21

Turning now to the newsy world the Red
Sox take last four claim pennant countries
taken in or out people counted no
count bombing voting mission killing
vision blurred our leader says God says
had hatred in his heart he said rage
testosterone he said our leader vote for God

22

God is not a Republican
Democrat Yankee Red
Sox fan of him or her—

But him is whom our bed
is holding, him my one is home
again, oh bless him keep him safe

this little time that is our life.

23

Lifetime, timeline, line-
up, down time, no time

to lose time, all time gone.

More of them, body count a full
count, bases loaded, all bets

off, one by one, or war
time lots, all at once.

24

Once there was a girl, a boy, end
of story in one first word, once

she was and nothing's left of her except

me oh my and her him too: her last

days he also came all back to me but

now my own him is here is not
once upon but times many.

25

Many, as in instances, or all,
one, as in passing, as in course of:

two words for time, in Vietnamese,
but one for all the times to do,
for go went gone, as in, this colder

day, the geese: only ducks and gulls
on the little pond, its tiny island.

26

Island's I, for all
the thinking not (no man
no self). Island's home,

at least for some. But here's
a little boat for back and forth

with one beside, rowing through
the eventide, the late evening.

27

Evening out. On
the town, out of town:

city wearing your black
dress sequined with lights, I

am coming down for an even-
ing out, in bed beside.

The rest: held by, holding.

28

Holding on the Red
Sox won eclipsing even the full

eclipsed moon a moment outside
the trouble we've seen though the TV had

to bring in the war the war that people
believe is good because they want
to believe it's a winning team

29

Teeming with leaves, trees
and ground all gold

around gray stones: I
am greeting my last
neighbors, we *shall*

all be changed, pieces
of gold slipping into air.

30

Airborne, air-born, hand-
sized cradle to hold
a soul, no broken-

bough fall. Good
news today, but best

in the air, this old
new leaf, turning it over.

31

Over and over again
and again, time

after time, stone
upon hallowed stone.

More than bones, ghost-
thin skin, I'm here, much

less less. Not yet not.

COMING THROUGH

COMING THROUGH

December 2005

1

Too old for calendar
toys, even half-
song's cracked

apart, one
will go before
the other, others come

2

None, he said,
is safe, numbers turn, click
open, shut—
        dreams keep us half-
alert, the last bird on the branch

turns to shift eyes, the last
eye always open

3

Sumac red, erect,
dead, shedding cattails

grayed, the last apples
fallen, browned, black

head above the water:
snake—no, stick

4

Snow lining branches hiding
even the stream it fills, no water

in the wilderness, no time to prepare
a way, valleys bombed and mountains
fortified, what comfort in the coming

here and we are going soon

5

No green fields below, only white
squares, brown we have drawn

upon our land, no mountains
rise, no seas, little trumpet in

the calendar square is silent only
rivers under ice are rushing on

6

Out of ice us: what
we're made of came from comets, which
are ice.
            Into ice some, the rest
to dust along with apples basket ladder only
seeds do something else,
                              oh one-
year-in-the-world grand-girl-and-boy

7

Drum today, the music
of war, drumming up business

for war, war for business, drummed
into all of us, drumfire's gunfire, rum-

pa-pa-pum is rat-a-tat-tat now boys
girls explode drumming themselves out

8

That day she sailed out
of this world, her sheets her sails, white,
raised,
          and the one she loved behind
her now, the ones,
                        their tiny boats
sailed off the churning sea
of the world as if over the edge

9

—and the alphabet of what
they were, *Oh!* in the diary, *B*
was here,

       the arithmetic of who
they were, three or two or one
unlearned,

        only words on the edge
of a desk, only one left to tell

10

and will not on the edge
of tell *(but did he at the end)*
say more—

       Think Snow striped by window
blinds *(remember her)*, think Under
the snow, think Bare branches nodding
yes yes but it is over

11

Not the light, not even the sudden
sun through the chapel window
as we sang the *Benedictus*, not

our voices but the hush
just after, stillness in the wilderness,
the comfort, hush of that voice

12

Deprived, I heard, not
surprised,
        but once I was, by him,
by joy, I am, by my
own one—
        Incarnation's One to call
all, that of God in two or three
or all together

13

One wasn't enough,
she needed another and then
another to make a self—

                  Tonight I trudged
through snow, hands in the garbage, a lost
book, whom to call, at last called
my own him, my one other

14

Because we are snow, snow
on bones, snow hearts with snow
veins branching out into stick
fingers,
         why should we need fires
explosions bombs since mere
sun comes soon enough?

15

They live in a palace a castle they think it good
for everyone that they should have more than most

For castles are made to defend it can only be better
if other castles are taken as if in a game

To play by the rules you've made may not be enough
if you live in a palace that someone else thinks good

16

Their bottle of Scotch, their bottles of beer, I took
them all, beer wine beer, as if we were playing a game

I hadn't explained, their stunned hands curved
around air where bottles had been, I took over

the party, my arms filled with seized green
clear brown, with senseless golden power

17

Green gone, only ever-s, ivies
twining anyway,
                    but the green-
less woods, straight, clean, with space
for sky,
            the clutter below covered
with snow, no ice except at the edge
of the creek, water
                        running through

18

He wanted a house so He found
a girl.
        He would fill the hungry with good
things, she said, herself a house filled
with good.
            He would empty the rich, the mighty
would fall through the seats of their own
. fine chairs.
            He would empty her and come through.

19

Love apple bird child
feast grass love-in-a-mist (white
flowers) love-lies-bleeding (red
spikes) less lorn lost—oh my own
of my life I am in with you trying
to make with give lovingkindness

20

In the Bible one year he underlined *love*
and its variations, he counted hundreds
of *loves, loveds, lovings, lovingk's*

He was her father and she
was my mother, he loved and counted
other words, he did not count the *nots*

21

If the forest fell
and no one heard only
a tree—
        We're winning
the war our big boy says we

we we all the way home
for the holidays and not counting

22

Just this, no
more
        low low cattle
lowing waking crows
cawing
        slow slow only
sheep, no angel, just
this at least my heart

23

Not enough
left, done:
              Tiny apples crushed
under the sidewalk ice:
                          This
is the end of myself as my-
self, I thought I could do
love, Love, but I . . .

24

I can: this is for you,
Love, the children, the babies
who came in winter, ice

hardens the snow,
Love, like us, but it shines
in the sun, that will be enough.

25

The baby
saves us after
            all from being
our hunger for more
than we can eat:
                arms must reach
out receive release hold back
from taking striking out against

26

I love you more
than I can say, she said

to me-become-everyone
her last year, *but I can tell*
you this:
            it's hard but it's good
and it's deep and it's forever.

27

as long as we both is not
long, my second person
singular, my one

sun in the morning, moon
going soon to that narrow bed
again, oh safe safe please keep him

28

hate may mean (no no) love love
may mean hate because we must

not hate but do because we must
may even want to die though not

just yet so guns not our arms
in place of love torture wounds

29

coming down to
you and me the wire
that separates us holds
us:
    I will hold on when they wound
to heal you soon, I will hold
you myself, first persons plural

30

bare branch bone
exposed line wire
down to the—
          flat off
key scratch this poor
thing cannot sing but
Love, here is my heart

31

Forever and ever as long
as we both: this is more
than a new year
                    —and suddenly
blue like a new season hope heart
light on the green-again ground
where life comes through

UNDER GREEN

UNDER GREEN

April 2006

1

April is the
first poem too
young for cruelest

time I wrote *when flowers*
wrote *rainbows* wrote *birds* too
young for memory then and

now is only just today my
love is well come home

2

first daffodils forsythia flash
the old gray world with grade
school yellow, scilla grounds
it blue, one tulip's red with yellow
pistil stamens still the same

3

Down the street from the green
school where lines form, the red
school waits
                    My love checks
his blood now, wet rubies
on his fingers
                    Love lives
on what is lost, draws
blood, colors us in

4

Hawk got dove
today. Sharp-shinned
hawk. Mourning dove. Beside
the garden pulled feathers, plucked
down, pecked at entrails wet with
blood, ate, flew low with
what was left— bird
heavy with bird

5

Sudden snow dusts ground,
maples red with early flowers,

snow turned rain will bring them
down, wash blood from broken

bodies, push up and out
green, out hidden leaves   .

6

Tulip closed against
the cold,
            snow bent it
down, made a smooth white
egg of it,
            its own heat
broke it open red

7

with him my love better
now each day break but
days do not begin end
break have never been
break so much with any
one break since I break
I hold will not break

8

Fifteen years, thousands of
days, millions of minutes
passed since that April

day when I, my own
one as-long-as-we-both-
live Love, said: Yes. Yes I do.

9

Days before, He came to the city
named for peace, where there was, where
there is, temple or mosque, no peace, riding
an ass or the colt of an ass, riding on branches
or clothes strewn in His path—
                                    But if the city
gates with different names, gates built on top of
gates, could lift their heads, if the stones,
bombed, refused, could rise together—

10

In the newly discovered good
news, the disciple named betrayer

is asked to sacrifice *the man
that clothes the master*: flesh

shed, not risen, death the good
gate to that which is no body

11

New seeds, red and green, male and female on one
tree, or meeting in air, buds like the buttons
that open the body—
                         But papery pale
beech leaves blaze the trail that leads
to the hill where just-dug graves—

12

tree gone willow
last winter fallen
taken stump hollow
hole now

and air where last
year vertical script
wrote early spring's
green news

13

Last year lambs, panicked by our
traffic, ran under their mothers, we

ate them later, we love the humble,
we eat and drink at the wooden table,

but the lamb was before the slaughter
of thousands in Egypt, and now in Eden

thousands, and bombs for the next
country, they say, war, we love that too.

14

Traffic halts, trees bleed
seeds beside the road,
reddened air, sudden

clouds, *Behold the time
is coming*, or is it come
this holy day of death?

15

April's more
red than green,
                    when I wrote at seven
the busy maple I didn't know what
the maple was doing,
                    but now I'm fixed
on magnolia: rose bullets on one side
of this tree and opening open-
ing open on the other

16

But would one want
one's body, made to make more
bodies, take, eat, heavy with bodies, would
one want one's body back?
                    Enough
the empty tomb, shed clothes, the lily, its open-
ing throat, broken shell, out and into
air that molds itself to all this is

17

Back through all that was before
I could meet you on the corner

I wrote, a second "April," another
you, but here we are, bodies not

the bodies they were, yours
healing, mine on hold, I thought

this would be for love, Love,
but it's body. Love's body.

18

hyacinths now, follow the scent, trees
white where they will be green, but
you walk more slowly now, and in
the woods we walk on what's
fallen, we walk on rot

19

Fallen, we say, but in war
movies we watch it's
bodies being

felled: in air

for a moment,
where, as if toward beds,
they fall back, breathless, taken

20

sweet showers   cruelest month
lilacs last   green endures   lines

drawn between pale green leaves
dotting trees and brown exposed

where there was snow, *mixed,* he said,
what we want with what we've had

21

Then, beneath the green cave, the red
room paled, I had no room, I wrote,
for anyone, was early done, but

you have opened a house, young
blood flushes my skin when come
sweet thoughts of your my body

22

Room in mind for body while
body rests, waits,
                    room in deeper
mind of dream for what's denied,
not recognized,
                    room if we re-
cognize, know over again each
other, for you and me, two
all day in this one house

23

Trout lilies shooting through
dead leaves stamens stretching
red pistil pushing yellow
up—
          You lying low then sitting
standing lying down again with me
all well again you are my spring

24

Nothing new in this green and
red, them and us, leaves sheer

like lingerie, deeper now, trees
crotched, deeper, roots—no,

we're not, we cannot root or
rise, we're crouched between

25

creeping phlox on an old
grave, someone's still coming up
through the stems of these rooted green
others, our distant relatives that
rise, start over and over

26

Touch skin to touch
muscle move blood find
bone
        to make blood
rise, blood held by veins
flesh skin
            to meet dear
body flesh Love not in blood
shed but in that clear
rush to see through body

27

Trees finding greens, coloring in
out to the edges, skeletal shadows
becoming shade, landscape painting
as it erases itself—
                              our lessened
bodies learning each day to be
what they are becoming

28

Out, or coming out,
dogwood, white and pink lace,
bride and her maid, lilacs breaking
their dark knots—
                              We are out on this
safe street, while a war, not broken out
but being made, is making more wars

29

still blue through half-
green trees and you
beside me now
safe, but

what are those
pale bee-y things
paused hawk-
like in our path?

30

Heavy with memory, this, old
Aprils, self with self, my,

it, lilac with lilac
will not fly—

But body still moves
to body, like to like or almost

like, even now I am learning
love in the school of desire

MOVING STILL

MOVING STILL

July 2007

1

Sun day summer day Sun-
day news & views more civilians

killed than soldiers Afghans around
their shoulders handsome dogs in these

our own United States so named on this
summer day our dogs bark but maybe some

day the sun the day the Lord hath made

2

Made in the day-old USA,
*by the Laws of Nature and Nature's
God*
        and then this morning the yolk
of the sun: full, I said, as if I spoke
of the moon,
                as if my country, our
country, wrote *all,* wrote *equal*—
Life, Liberty and the pursuit

3

pursuit of happiness guaranteed
by much of the paper, ads for more

designer purses perfume shoes
for some of the people, those

who can, for us this summer
ocean bed view love our

summer's not for all

4

all are created equal endowed by Creator

while they were finishing midday prayers

bombs bursting in fireworks bombs

charred bodies had no faces

bright stars the rockets red

could not protect

our Lives our sacred Honor

5

Honor the sun that sheds the light
that falls upon us, honor the clouds
that gather and make the rain
that falls upon us, honor the earth
that holds and keeps us, honor
That Which made us, gave us
honor, the sun, the hurting earth.

6

Earth: mantled mother big
blue marble pale blue dot not

blue until we got out there we
thought talked green forgot

the water now we let green
go cut it burn it turn it into

stuff, junk, shall her bones live?

7

Live from our own
dawn air, featuring song
sparrow, cardinal, mourning

dove, alive and well
in our bed my love, his slow
sleeping breathing, low continuo

entered into this summer score

8

Score one for sea, one for sky, blue
meets blue, line, tie,
                one for sand,
now exposed, turning tide,
leaving sand,
            birds for all, least
terns hover, dart, piping
plovers scurry,
            can we all agree
with these on earth sea sky?

9

Sky items: Yesterday I disturbed
the nesting terns, they charged
like planes,
            in May the osprey flew
away from the camera raised
to count eggs,
            today NATO planes
killed 105 in a village, today
clouds, then rain, then—

10

Then he said *love* and by
that summer we were settled

months before the Wall fell and we
said *peace*, years before the Towers
fell and we said *war* Iraq Iraq Iraq

Afghanistan Darfur how to save
what's been lost oh little world

11

World's with *us, we*

are world, 6.6 billion, 194 countries not
counting, 19 major religions not counting—

conflicts across borders shifting indefinite
porous unmanaged within among
stateless races religions cultures—

Earth's with or without us, was never center.

12

Centered, surrounded by pines, one
could forget the uncentered world

except for the parallel cables and wires
scratching the landscape, the cloudless sky,

stretching all the way to a vest strapped
to a six-year-old boy who is told that flowers
will spray out if he touches, here, this button.

13

Button of bird, ribbon
of song sparrow notes
and trill, notes and trill, over
and over,
          early sun jeweling
the pines, gilding the sea beyond
the pines,
          news to come of
news of over and over

14

Over time, the President says, sustained
period, time is not right, progress
is being made—
          No creation without
destruction, said Anaximander, everything
moves, nothing remains—
          But must that mean
no Revolution without Terror, no peace
without creating more reasons for war?

15

wars and rumours of wars

flag and (un)furling of flag

body and breaking of body

bone and gnawing of bone

earth and (re)turn to earth

birds and songs of birds

sun and rising of sun

16

Sun at the center, even when, through a wound
in deep blue clouds, ooze of pink becoming
the clouds, sea of pink above our own
tinged sea, from a slash of fire, it seems,
as onto a stage, as in the tabernacle He made
for it, to rise, fire itself, red then gold, laying
a shimmering path on our sea, our star the sun.

17

Sun was moving around again:
Copernicus spurned, Bruno burned
The world is stablished it cannot be moved

But Galileo looked through a telescope, found
the Milky Way was stars, Jupiter had moons,
earth had to move. Mathematics,

he said, is the language which God . . .

18

God-named, they named
our days, those wandering
stars, and then we were one

too, moving between Love
and War, making love war (bit
off her lip), war love (came

to kill), making our days.

19

Daily Meditations . . . Begun July 19, 1666.
By Philip Pain: Who lately suffering
Shipwrack, was drowned: the first
published American verse: *This World*
a Sea of trouble is . . . . *The billows beat,*
the waves are angry, he wrote the first
day of *Quotidian Preparations for Death.*

20

Deaths of civilians hit by convoys,
shot at checkpoints: the open hand
they thought meant *Come!* meant *Stop!*

. . . his open hand, my closed-around-
him hand, our more-than-hands . . .

600,000 civilians, British doctors say,
almost a third by coalition, ours

21

Our summer house, key under the mat

On the porch, his children's girl
and boy, their little trucks and cars

On the ledge, robins nesting again

On the tiny stones that are sand,
generations of waves in a minute,
castles and forts washed daily away

22

Away from the roof where we sit

streamers of rose silver gold, west

and east, sunset pinks the whole sky

The Lord is a man of war: the Lord is His name

But: *He maketh wars to cease, to the end of the earth*

The earth the Lord has made, this into-light

The breaking of the surf, the mourning dove

23

Dove each morning, sun, my love
beside me in our summer bed

beside me in our afternoon

Can we love well our own
without owning the world?

My love, well, each night

o moon   *oh oh*

24

o o, no *no*, no *a*, no *the*

being nothing's some-
thing else: *nothing's*
peace, blessèd

(one lone loon)

if of mind perhaps
between perhaps among

25

Among the fledged terns testing
their wings, over the sand,
                              between
breaking waves with shining
heads of seals *up down up* and
cliff with bas-relief of little
hills carved by the sea,
                         we walk
a little while, our little while.

26

While we were sleeping, earth
was moving, earth as planet, earth

as element, earth as dirt
in my hands, my hands as dirt.

Body heart soul prepared to go
with pitch pine, chickadee, but how

to prepare for the death of all, the earth?

27

earth as it is

in heaven: sky
on sky, better country,

stars as they are:

more than we knew: space-
time, all one, at once, uni-
multiverse, Amen.

28

Amen before the heretics burned, before
the white was hanged but not the black.

We can't just bomb them, she said
into her cellphone, standing beside
the trendy shop, *we have to annihilate them.*

The mathematics of war: not x
not equals, naught for naught.

29

Not only the dead Monarchs
on the beach, lashed
by the waves,
                    or the gray
clouds passing over, clouding
the page of white clouds,
                              but
also, for a moment, an O of sun,
nothing, oh! silvering sea

30

Seeing things is changing things
I wrote, meaning Better, but could
be worse, not to mention blur—

Blink, shift, and the white tiles
become black, the black white

We work in the dark, we do . . .

our poor eyes, our little lights

31

Light's given, earth receives, *beside
me in our summer,* through her cover,

thinned, holed. Earth's disturbed.

But *eppur si muove*: whether,
recanting, he said it or not,

our earth still moves, is moving
still, around, and around our sun.

AFTER WORK

AFTER WORK

September 2008

1

Rest for all who labor, work for, build
our houses, pave our streets, nurse
the fallen on our streets, those

who cannot anymore, not one
day off but all shut out unhoused
upon our streets unnursed unheard

in this our country's right to work—

2

went to work when he was five

school   work   school   work

and then a wife a child—

camera now: first day of school

new clothes / shoes smile   smile

and then he quit his good job

and then he was not then

3

He was not minding
his store or the small

wood desk that now
was his store. 'Intensive

care,' said the girl who sat
in his place at the desk.

Intensive. Girl in his place.

4

In pots in baskets in place
of summer rust bronze burnt

sienna dusty purple colors
muted except for yellow

sun an urgent heat
breezed to keep us wanting

more when less is soon—

5

The day when less
slowed to none, last

breath out, machine
shut down, his death

day twenty years ago
was Labor Day, he labored

long and would not anymore.

6

Too hot for, would not want
to, blossoms drop, weeds
droop, seeds do not—

but still a ways to go,
a way: my own *work*
is play I wrote, though later

changed *word play* to *word work*

7

changed word line life leaf
on the street still green
edges browned

chickadee's little
song no *dee dee dee*

little losses bones cuts

evening morning glory closing up

8

Queen Anne's lace closing up
into seedy cups, goldenrod
going to greenish beads

purple beads of pokeweed
bled from deep pink stems

above the field a field
of mist those mornings

9

This morning fields
of clouds, fields coming out

of the clouds, squares, circles
in squares, browns, tans bound
by lines, north to south, east

to west where we
are going in unmarked air—

10

Going into this different land-
scape, as into someone else's

house: adobe walls, hills dotted
with deep green, ground brushed

with yellow chamisa, sun-
flowers, purple asters—

Deep green that will not change

11

will or will not fall
again: our towers walls
or fall that sudden way
again not down but in
and all within ash bone
dust and all the others
fallen after shot bombed

12

as if he had fallen after he quit

his job no job a lesser job and then his small

American dream: the drugstore where he'd worked at ten

become an immaculate pharmacy:

his own, with matching bottles, jars

but barely made our living, six long days—

then sold the store   then the old dreaming

13

called the number, the old
house number, hadn't spoken
for days, at last a Voice:

'They're not here, Sunshine,'
and saw the empty blue
bins and knew I'd heard

Whom I'd heard for the first time

14

The first time I lost a familiar
word was when my friend lost
something I'd never used:

tiny house for one, you
you *uterine* lost, only *can-*
cer remembered, end-
ing not beginning.

15

-ing: not yet not, as

in here, water trickling
in the riverbed, the prickly

pear agave cholla come
from somewhere else:

endless sand with empty
water bottles, bodies

16

more bombs bodies targets
missed, will we vote

for more war God's-
plan war just war just

wrong, *We are Egypt, we
are Rome*, said the minister, *we*

are empire, against the world

17

against the poor the working
poor the work deprived the
immigrant different tan
Hispanic black red terrorist
alien yellow all the same not
white not us see white
papers my white papers pink

18

every day his white shirt bow tie

at home writing letters for dreamed-of work

finally part-time substitute

small-town drugstore rooming house

—and then a downtown pharmacy, a small

success: a store he could manage like his own

till knees weak at seventy he retired

19

At seventy, retired, my love,
who has not been in this poem

before, is safe and well, he reads
and naps in another room
and loves me better than any

one and waits, we wait
for another baby to come

20

Still to come: years: yellow
leaves still few as fruits
on these tough green
Siberian elms but

when yellower aspens
stir the warm wind I start
to count from the other end.

21

Into the other side
of town we ride in the back
seat, streets narrowed

by windowless concrete
walls, windshield covered
with thick paper, driver

speaking a language no one knows

22

stories no one knows anymore, his,
hers, but early today, her birth-
day, *she handed me some pages*
while I slept *and asked, 'Could*
you translate these for me?' and then
I boarded the little plane we prayed
could get through the rough weather

[85]

23

Baby came through the door
of his tiny house last night

out of the water into
the air into the room

rooms room door
after door, huge new house

with no ceiling except the sky

24

ceilinged walled but not
yet boxed, retired but not

retiring, right now get
to work, right to work, I—

or they, who cannot, have not:

ceilinged down floored Wall-
Streeted out wronged worked out

25

in and out of work he worked: people were

his work, he said: doctors met in his one

good job, customers helped in the stores

sick kids pregnant women ex-addicts a prostitute

and later in the grocery cleaners coffee shop

people he met, kids he told to stay in school—

good work, my good father, good Will

26

Hoped it good, Father, hoped it true
to your last words, *This could be
a better place*, to tell the hard parts—

Today, awake, I did not see
as one in old memories sees, but felt
myself against your starched shirt, you

holding me and all you believed I might be

27

holding me my love yes but some
times as with him I forget seem
to think myself the sun around
which in some distant or closer
buzzing around my head my
hand batting away—but needed him
to start / need you to keep me going

28

nothing to keep:
adobe crumbles scrub
oak juniper pinyon jay

hawk crow squawk of what
will not word urn bits
of tagged bone star-

laced darkness that clothes air

29

The clothes have come out
of their houses, dresses, jackets lit

the colors of embers, or monarchs: they
are flying like butterflies and now

the houses are also flying: transparent
except for those that have gathered
blue sky into themselves

30

Beyond blue: absence
containing contained

On the road crows consume
a lizard. All in a day's—

All consuming the road before us.

Work, for the night is coming. Work
after work. Work, for the night

GRAYED IN

GRAYED IN

January 2009

1

Snow fallen, another going
gone, new come in, open
the door:
        each night I grow
young, my friends are well
again, my life is all
before me,
        each morning
I close a door, another door.

2

Cloud on cloud, gray
on gray, snow fallen

on snow, tree on tree
on unleafed tree—

only a river silvered
with thin ice and a slash
of gold in the late gray sky.

3

Grayed snow slush trudge but

snow falling coating filling

in for absence *Present!*

child with stringed mittens

here to take her place

to take over on

snow showing up air

4

White sky, whiter sun brushing
trees with tints of red, then

in the distance streaking
mauve gold, filling in
between the now filagreed

trees, silhouettes against
the now red burning sky.

5

As if letting go, dangling down,
only down, through a cracked
pane, a clear pane, weeping
beech branches, roots

in air, only the crack slant-
ing up or (last night in sleep's
play a long red slide) sloping down

6

down buildings walls houses
schools, no one building only

bombing, months of little in,
now nothing no one out, only

down: bodies arms legs in Gaza

where the eyeless man tore pillars
house himself the people down

7

On this day, this birthday, I wish
myself for the first time (who
would be a child again?) back

at that dining room table with
him, his years of little more less
back, not as in the note in her

birthday book, *died 84 yrs of age*

8

snow	rain	ice
stand	walk	fall
little	more	less
face	flesh	hand
will	is	was
oh	yes	no
melt	rain	snow

9

Off the page, sliding or
I brush or don't see
you, but without
you, so cold, colder
than stooped-by-age
shoulder, oh flesh, hand,
Love, come turn my page.

10

Tempered by age, passion, rage
cool, no lost sleep—
                    while in sleep
they burn again, your fine hand
igniting my thigh, live birds
crushed under my feet,
                    then
morning grays again, aged
back, writing *died . . . of age*

11

As body to body fall-
ing together we burn
again, snow drifts
in air, turns, rolls
almost horizontal,
takes its own slow
time off from falling

12

Gun to body, shell to body, bombs
to bodies:
            three, five, now nine
hundred bodies, over two hundred
children's bodies,
                over the border
to Gaza to close the already closed
border,
        not to meet, border to border:
·a border has no body, is only a side.

13

Epiphany missed, *not the seen but the coming*

to see, or star, the minister said, light sensed

against the dark, but not even the dark

night, or the cold bright, snow

roof over the roof below the darkness

before— only gray, industrial gunmetal

battleship slate gray, and the coming of gray

14

Friend Sleep has betrayed me I'm trapped
in a castle with villainess villain two
doors open a third slams down before
the darkness I'm trapped in a room my
friends accuse me I hide my sheets I cannot
tell them I'm dying and then awaking I'm
hurting *(why these dreams?)* my betraying self

15

In sleep a holocaust rations trapped
in a kitchen ovens coming *why not eat*
them if food is scarce—
                    In Gaza food
is scarce, power lost, the UN Compound,
a hospital hit today, now over 1000 dead—

But see, here, *History: the Future*: some
hope, though still rationed, is Coming Soon.

16

stuck zipper sticky egg
wiped off mouth mother's

mouth lined around but
pursed now closer why

not eat touch again all
right merge again then

zip: put sleep to sleep

17

Today the train *too fast*
they said *too soon* they
said *not yet* they said

to Washington all
right now a black
man to the White

House on the train.

18

On his way to the Capitol largely built by slaves
who baked bricks, cut, laid stone—
                                on his way
to stand before the Mall where slaves were held
in pens and sold—
                        on his way to a White
House partly built by slaves, where another
resident, after his Proclamation, wrote:
If slavery is not wrong, nothing is wrong.

19

One hundred years later, King said
and said to the crowd on the Mall,
Now is the time and *We can never
be satisfied as long as,* he

dreamed: *every valley
exalted,* all these years until
not an end, they said, *a beginning*

20

O bless hold help keep
him safe, let him help
us through this cold,

let us help him help
us through this
cold, let its end be

O yes a beginning.

21

Cold is in the air, troops are finally out
of Gaza where 1300 dead are on or in
the ground where olive trees are up-
rooted, down, spoons a coloring
book limbs shoes in the rubble—

In the depths of winter, he said.

Today he is In, at work.

22

White roof over the roof, white
branches clinging to branches, even
the still fallen snow is moving, even
icicles shift toward dripping, nothing,
not even the cold bodies we are
becoming is not moving, not even
the ground is not moving, over, on

23

Beyond my windowed
wall, gray clouds move over
clouds,
          beyond the Wall
that grays Gaza, dust
over dust of disturbed
bodies,
          wall with drawn-
in windows, winter mirror

24

cold	heart	comfort	shoulder
feet	hands	water	drawn
in	from	left	out
take	stay	sober	stone
grave	still	body	turn
on	light	open	to
warm	up	front	heart

25

fallen snow shifts
blows drifts from tree
to ground, leaves
the beautiful skeletal
limbs open to only
all over air wind
lifts then lets fall

26

He stumbled but still, she blundered
but still, they said what they shouldn't
have said and recovered, of course

they are the great but even the small
(though all, we early learn, may fall)
may leave the mistaken, misspoken

behind as late we stumble into our selves.

27

maybe not long, you said,
cancer cancer cancer, c's
crashing like waves—

waves of frozen foam
that day on that lake—

you who please don't go I
can late we I can better Love I

28

mouth with you to mouth
with you to body with you
in body embodied, not yet un-

bodied Love I can better no
room so warm as *with*—

I think I thought I could I
can but not without you

29

In Vietnam: new year of the water buffalo,
steady, slow, welcomed with peach
blossoms, fruits, red wine—

In Gaza: year of the new
war, now ended but no room to bury
the dead, no place for the living

to buy food, water, any . . .

30

for the woman who cooks
on a fire of sticks, her bag
of clothes on a tree

for those going home
to water their trees, lemon
and almond and olive

and for those trees

31

snow to rain to ice to melt to

freeze frame window grayed

in with old self same but

new has come can better

Love I— going home bless keep

clean gray slate not white or black for

even these few words, this small rain

ACKNOWLEDGMENTS

Philip Pain's *Daily Meditations and Quotidian Preparations for Death* was first published in 1668; according to the facsimile edition issued by the Huntington Library in 1936, it is "the earliest known specimen of original American verse printed in the English Colonies." Each day for sixteen days in 1666, Pain wrote four six-line meditations, followed by a couplet.

"Over Time" is indebted to www.moonshop.com (see section 5), where deeds to "lunar properties" are available.

"Coming Through" utilizes a children's Advent calendar, in which twenty-four "doors," one for each day of Advent, open onto pictures of toys, or images related to the Christmas season and story. Liturgical readings for the Sundays of Advent and Christmas, including the Magnificat (see section 18), are also incorporated into the poem.

"Under Green" utilizes liturgical readings for Palm Sunday, Maundy Thursday, Good Friday, and Easter. The discovery and translation of the apocryphal Gospel of Judas was announced during this period (see section 10).

"Moving Still" is indebted to the *New York Times, Boston Globe, The Nation*, Dava Sobel, the Bible, and Henry James, among others.

"Grayed In" is indebted to the *New York Times*, *Guardian (UK)*, and *New Statesman*, among other news sources, as well as (beyond their quoted words) to Abraham Lincoln and Martin Luther King, Jr.

"Over Time" first appeared in *Boulevard*, "Coming Through" in *Pleiades*, "Under Green" in *Epiphany*, "After Work" in *Prairie Schooner*, and "Moving Still" and "Grayed In" in the *Seattle Review*. My thanks to the editors of these publications, and to the University of Pittsburgh Press, where three sections of "Grayed In" appeared in my book *White Papers* (2012).

My thanks also to the friends who read these poems over the years, and to Jen Liu, who (I remembered long after I had begun this work) completed a similar sequence in December 1997.

MARTHA COLLINS is the author of six volumes of poetry, including *White Papers* (Pittsburgh, 2012) and the book-length poem *Blue Front* (Graywolf, 2006). She has also published three collections of co-translated Vietnamese poetry—most recently *Black Stars: Poems by Ngo Tu Lap* (Milkweed, 2013, with the author). Her awards include fellowships from the NEA, the Bunting Institute, and the Witter Bynner Foundation, as well as an Anisfield-Wolf Award, two Ohioana Awards, the Laurence Goldstein Poetry Prize, and three Pushcart Prizes. Founder of the Creative Writing Program at UMass-Boston, she served as Pauline Delaney Professor of Creative Writing at Oberlin College until 2007, and is currently editor-at-large for *FIELD* magazine and one of the editors of the Oberlin College Press.

Interior design by Gretchen Achilles / Wavetrap Design
Typeset in Dante
by Gretchen Achilles / Wavetrap Design